B.C. on the Rocks

Johnny Hart

CORONET BOOKS
Hodder Fawcett, London

Copyright © 1966, 1967 by
Publishers News Syndicate Inc.
Copyright © 1971 by Fawcett Publications Inc.

First published 1971 by Fawcett Publications Inc.,
New York

Coronet edition 1974
Second impression 1975
Third impression 1977

Printed in Great Britain for
Hodder Fawcett Ltd.,
Mill Road, Dunton Green, Sevenoaks, Kent
(Editorial Office: 47 Bedford Square,
London, WC1 3DP)
by Hazell Watson & Viney Ltd,
Aylesbury, Bucks

ISBN 0 340 18820 0

.. ADDING PROOF TO THE RUMOR THAT SUZIE SPOTLESS HAS SPLIT FOR MEXICO WITH SMOKEY THE BEAR.

hart

CLAMP

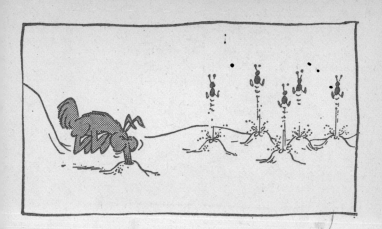

SLUUP

I NEGLECTED TO CONSIDER THE LAW OF SUCTION.

GROG

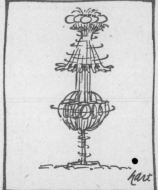

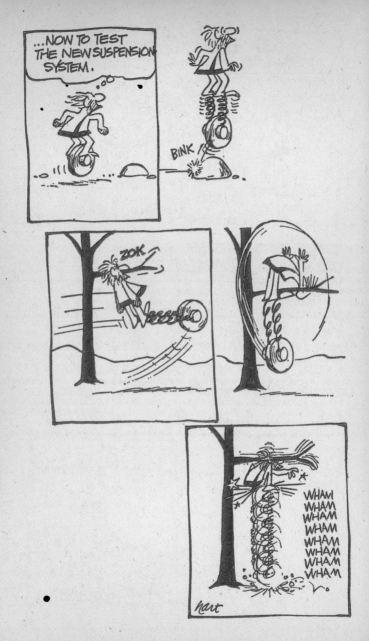

HOW 'BOUT A PIGGY-BACK RIDE?

HOW BOUT THAT.

GROG

WHY DID YOU DIG THIS HOLE IN THE FIRST PLACE ?
TO CATCH A WORM!
THAT'S RIGHT, ...I FORGOT.
AAAAAAAA
LOOK! ....IT'S A WORM!
YOU EAT IT... I'M NOT HUNGRY.
hart

ZIP

hart

hart.

GOT ALL YOUR GIFT SHOPPING DONE?
ALL EXCEPT FOR THE STINKING QUEEN.
IF YOU DON'T LIKE THE QUEEN, WHY DO YOU BUY HER GIFTS?
SO SHE WON'T FIND OUT.
hart

GLOMP

MUNCH
MUNCH
MUNCH
MUNCH

PTUI

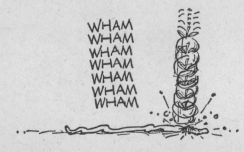

sets us apart from others.

rēward' v.t.
something you get—

for doing something
you wouldn't ordinarily do—

if it wasn't for the reward.

lăn'guage *n.* a combination of sounds emitted through an orifice in the front of the skull.

often to the discomfort-

of the two aperatures on the sides of the skull.

hart

nothing *n.*

tree. *n.* any of a
number of giant
fruit bearing –

and/or leafy plants.

(RARE. *found in housing
developments.*)

rock (RŎK) *n.*

to cause something
or someone to sway–

by hitting them with it.

hart

lēad'er *n.* a person who makes an important decision,

then sits back,

and answers stupid questions for the rest of his life.

hart

hip *n.* that broad part
of the body—

on which the hands
rest in anger.

especially on women.

nŏn'sense * n.

WHAT DOES IT MEAN
WHEN A "*" APPEARS
AFTER A WORD?

IT MEANS SOMEBODY
CLOSED THE BOOK ON
A BUG.

bōne *n.* one of a group of moving parts—

which moved too slowly—

to avoid being buried by a dog.

in which mudballs are trump.